I0190225

HE WOULD RATHER DIE THAN LIVE WITHOUT YOU

HE WOULD RATHER DIE THAN LIVE WITHOUT YOU

Exploring the Love of Christ
and What it Means to
Be a Christian

BONNY V. BANKS

He Would Rather Die Than Live Without You
Steward Publishing, Lake Hopatcong, New Jersey

Unless otherwise noted, scripture quotations are taken from the Holy Bible, New Living Translation, copyright © 1996, 2004, 2007 by Tyndale House Foundation. Used by permission of Tyndale House Publishers, Inc., Carol Stream, Illinois 60188. All rights reserved. Scripture quotations marked (KJV) are from the Holy Bible, Authorized King James Version. Belgium: Thomas Nelson Publishers 2001. Used by permission. We have taken creative license to apply or decline the use of capital lettering where deemed appropriate.

Copyright © 2012 by Bonny V. Banks

All rights reserved. No part of this book may be reproduced, stored in a retrieval system, scanned or transmitted, in any form or by any means, electronic, mechanical, photocopying, recording or otherwise, without the prior written permission of the publisher. Please do not participate in or support piracy of copyrighted materials in violation of the author's rights. Purchase only authorized editions.

Requests for permission to use or reproduce material from this book should be directed to:
Permissions@StewardPublishiing.com.

Library of Congress Cataloguing-in-Publication Data

Banks, Bonny V.
He Would Rather Die Than Live Without You/ Bonny V. Banks
    ISBN-13: 978-0-9796106-6-0

Printed in the United States of America
The paper used in this publication meets the requirements of the American National Standard for Permanence of Paper for Publication and Documents in Libraries and Archives 239.48-1992

Dedication

To my sister, Sharon.
You live to see the whole world experience
the healing love of Jesus Christ

You live the song,

*"This little light of mine,
I'm gonna let it shine…"*

Acknowledgments

Bless You, Father,
You are my heart.

Thank you for my parents,
Lonnie Jr. and Emma, who gave me life and
introduced me to You.

Thank you for Jeffery,
whose life reflects Your mantra
and Jesus' heart's song,
"It's all about mercy."

Thank you, for my Bishop,
Phillip F. Cargile, Sr.
"Jesus is Lord, The Lord, He is God and
God is our Father."

Thank you for my first Pastor,
Rev. Mother Derris Cargile,
"Thank God for Jesus and the Plans of Salvation."

Table of Contents

Dedication... v

Acknowledgments... vii

Perfect Love 1

Who is God and Who Am I to Him? 3

The Plan of Salvation.. 11

The Sin Problem 15

How Did We Get Here?.............................. 15

Who Is Jesus and Why Do I Need Him? 31

Your New Life in Christ 49

Choosing a Church Home........................... 49

Who is the Holy Spirit? 50

A Word About Faith 67

Guard Your Gates 73

Focus On God's Approval 85

Perfect Love

"For God so loved the world, that He gave His only begotten Son, that whosoever believeth in Him should not perish, but have everlasting life."

- Jesus Christ

"What love is this that gave so freely that I, the guilty one, may go free?"
- Graham Kendrick

Imagine a love that thinks of you every minute of every day and never tires of reassuring you. Imagine a love so complete that every empty space in your heart is filled. Imagine a love that cares about everything that concerns you. Imagine a love that is always present, never far away and always has time for you. Imagine a love that only wants the best for you, a love that defends you, protects you, provides for you and rejoices over you. Imagine a love that affectionately longs to spend time with you, generously gives to you and is always interested in what you have to say. Imagine a love that is constant no matter what you do. Imagine a love that seeks to save you and spend all eternity with you. Imagine a love that would rather die than live without you.

That is the love that Jesus Christ has for you. Jesus loves you with an everlasting love, a love that will never fade, a love that will never separate from you. The love that Jesus has for you is unlike any you could ever experience with another person because Jesus' love is perfect.

People try to be good and loving and caring, but because of the frailties of merely being human, people fall short of perfection. That is why your human heart still cries out for more even when there are special people all around who express their love for you. There is a space within the human heart that I believe God has reserved just for Himself. Until we let Jesus Christ into that intimate place something within us remains unfulfilled. Once we accept Jesus Christ as our Lord and Savior our hearts somehow find fulfillment and satisfaction heretofore unknown. It is as if our souls are at peace. It is like finding our way back home after being lost for a long, long time.

You may ask yourself, 'How can God truly love me?' The answer to that question is quite simple. God loves you because He created you. God is love and God's love is unconditional. Because God created you, He knows everything about you, even those things you may not be so proud of and wish you could change. With God it is not about earning or deserving His love. God loves you because you are His. God sees value in you. Think of your love for your children. You may disagree with some of their behaviors or ways of thinking, but your love is always there. Even when you are apart from your children, you cannot forget them. You are God's child. He created you for the joy of being Your Heavenly Father and He will always love and think of you, even when He disagrees with some of your behavior. God loves you because you belong to Him.

As hard as it may be to imagine anyone capable of such love, consider Jesus. Jesus died in your place so you would not have to live a life void of fellowship with God and all eternity without redemption. Now that is love. You see, when God created Adam, God blew the breath of life into Adam and Adam became a living soul. The Bible tells us in Genesis chapter 2 verse 7, *"Then the Lord God formed the man from the dust of the ground. He breathed the breath of life into the man's nostrils, and the man became a living person."*

Who is God and Who Am I to Him?

God *is*. As simple and profound as it reads, God just is. There are not words adequate enough in the human lexicon to describe God who is indescribable.

Jesus said that God is Spirit. *"God is spirit [the Source of life, yet invisible to mankind], and those who worship Him must worship in spirit and truth"* (John 4:24, Amplified Version, AMP).

God is eternal. God had no beginning and He has no end. God was not born or created. God is and will always be. God does not live in time, God created time for humankind. God's word is eternal, God's promises are eternal and God's love is eternal.

When God breathed into Adam making Adam a living person, Adam came alive forever, literally. In the same way, every person and generation since Adam, including you and me, were created as living beings that will never die for all eternity. You ask, How could that be possible?

God is Spirit and God created you in His image and likeness. You are a spirit.

> *Then God said, "Let Us (Father, Son, Holy Spirit) make man in Our image, according to Our likeness [not physical, but a spiritual personality and moral likeness]; and let them have complete authority over the fish of the sea, the birds of the air, the cattle, and over the entire earth, and over everything that creeps and crawls on the earth* (Genesis 1:26, AMP).

You are a spirit. You have a soul. You live in a body.

After God created time (marked by day and night), God formed the first man, Adam, from the dust of the ground. Adam did not come alive until God breathed into Adam. God is Spirit and it is

God's Spirit that God breathed into Adam, the being God had formed out of the dust of the ground.

Because God is eternal, when God breathed into Adam, Adam became a living spirit with a soul that will never die. The essence of who you are as a living being will never become non-existent. Your flesh and mine, because of Adam's sin, are destined to return to the earth from whence it came, but our souls are alive forever. It is impossible for the eternity of God, which God breathed into Adam for all succeeding generations, to be constrained by mortality.

Before Adam sinned, Adam would have lived forever as flesh and blood on the earth, but when Adam sinned by disobeying God, Adam brought about death to the human body and everlasting separation from God to every soul. Consider what the Bible says about Adam's sin. *"When Adam sinned, sin entered the world. Adam's sin brought death, so death spread to everyone, for everyone sinned"* (Romans 5:12).

When Adam disobeyed God, Adam brought upon himself and every person after him, including you and me, what the Bible calls a sin nature. A sin nature is the natural desire to do that which conflicts with the will of God. Selfishness and the desire to give in to every fleshly desire are part of the sin nature. This is the reason you and I need Jesus.

You see, we often say we are not perfect and rightly so. We are not. No person is sinless. Every human being on earth commits sin, whether consciously, unconsciously or both every day. There is no way to escape the sin nature and completely cease from sinning against God, no matter how hard we try. The Psalmist, David, summed it up for us all. *"For I was born a sinner - yes, from the moment my mother conceived me"* (Psalm 51:5).

Have you ever tried to keep the Ten Commandments? When God gave Moses the Ten Commandments, people tried but failed in keeping them. Even in Jesus' day, religious scholars called Pharisees and Scribes tried in vain to present themselves as people who were perfect at keeping *The Law*, but to no avail. Knowing what was really going on in their hearts, Jesus pointed out the Pharisees and Scribes' hypocrisy, not because Jesus wanted to condemn anyone, but to free the people who had been struggling to live up to the standard these Pharisees and religious teachers had imposed.

On one occasion, Jesus said to those who boasted in keeping *The Law*, *"How terrible it will be for you teachers of religious law and you Pharisees. Hypocrites! You are like whitewashed tombs - beautiful on the outside but filled on the inside with dead people's bones and all sorts of impurity"* (Matthew 23:27).

God, knowing that the sin nature would always prevent humankind from living a sinless life, chose to create salvation for us by becoming the perfect sacrifice for sin. God says in His word, *"For this is how God loved the world: He gave his one and only Son, so that everyone who believes in him will not perish but have eternal life. God sent his Son into the world not to judge the world, but to save the world through him"* (John 3:16-17).

The Pharisees and Scribes lived among people who thought righteousness or right standing with God could be accomplished by good behavior and following rules. The problem was then as it is today that the sin nature prevents human beings from living victoriously over sin apart from Christ.

How many times have you said or thought to yourself, 'I am going to get right with God?' Jesus pointed out that while it may be possible to demonstrate proper outward behaviors or observe religious customs, God cares most about what is going on our hearts. Consider this illustration Jesus gave His disciples.

> *Two men went to the Temple to pray. One was a Pharisee, and the other was a despised tax collector. The Pharisee stood by himself and prayed this prayer: 'I thank you, God, that I am not a sinner like everyone else. For I don't cheat, I don't sin, and I don't commit adultery. I'm certainly not like that tax collector! I fast twice a week, and I give you a tenth of my income.'*

"But the tax collector stood at a distance and dared not even lift his eyes to heaven as he prayed. Instead, he beat his chest in sorrow, saying, 'O God, be merciful to me, for I am a sinner.' I tell you, this sinner, not the Pharisee, returned home justified before God. For those who exalt themselves will be humbled, and those who humble themselves will be exalted (Luke 18:10-14).

The Pharisee in this parable had it all wrong. There is no way that any of us can deserve God's grace. God, knowing the weakness of humankind and humankind's inability to live sinless lives, sent His Son, Jesus, to show us the way to the Father's heart. The way to the Father's heart is to open our hearts to Jesus.

Jesus' purpose in coming into the world was to take your place and mine in dying for our sins. Jesus did not come to condemn us for our sin, but to save us from the power and penalty of sin. Jesus paid the price for your sin so you do not have to.

People who reject Jesus chose to pay their own price for their sin. This results in being forever separated from God for all eternity because only a sinless soul can condemn sin and stand before a holy God. Just as working on a job earns one a paycheck, living a life of sin has its rewards - death and eternal separation from God.

According to God's word, the debt for sin had to be paid through death. *"The law of Moses was unable to save us because of the weakness of our sinful nature. So God did what the law could not do. He sent his own Son in a body like the bodies we sinners have. And in that body God declared an end to sin's control over us by giving his Son as a sacrifice for our sins"* (Romans 8:3).

Jesus Christ, God's only begotten Son, lived a completely sinless life and would have escaped death because of it. But, choosing instead to accept death and Hell for you and me, Jesus, being innocent, died and in return you and me, the guilty, are given the opportunity to escape our much deserved punishment for our sin. Romans 6:23 tells us, *"For the wages of sin is death, but the free gift of God is eternal life through Christ Jesus our Lord."*

The Plan of Salvation

"And ye shall know the truth, and the truth shall make you free."
                                                    - Jesus Christ

There is much that can be said about the mysterious nature of God and His plan for humankind's redemption. It may seem difficult to comprehend, but God created each of us with an innate ability to believe in His existence. Humankind all around the world from the beginning of time understood that there is something, better yet, *Someone* higher than a human being who controls the universe and all the laws of nature, including life and death.

The human conscience may be the single most indicator of creation. Without going to church or reading a Bible, each individual person knows right from wrong somehow. There is something within the human heart that knows it is right to treat others as one wishes to be treated.

While cultures vary and as such tend to inform patterns of behavior, human beings are born with an internal pointer that lets one know when one's words, actions, thoughts or behaviors have violated the unspoken rule of treating others as one wishes to be treated. Have you ever had a guilty conscience about something you thought, said, did or omitted doing? The human conscience is what drives heartfelt and sincere apologies, regrets, earnest change and sometimes, self-destructive behaviors.

The human conscience, although it enlightens and informs our understanding of right and wrong or morality as it is called, cannot be explained by science or anything we can observe physically. While science can explain the dividing of living cells and procreation to an extent, science cannot explain *why* we are here or *how* we know right from wrong. Further, science cannot explain how right and wrong came into being or why these innate perceptions exist.

There is a not so modern concept called *relativism* which suggests that there is no definite right or wrong and that each individual on the earth gets to decide individually what is right or wrong. Some call it living in one's individual truth. Relativism, however, cannot explain how or why thoughts and feelings of right and wrong exist. Relativism falls short of explaining the shared human knowing that to treat others justly and with fairness is right and good.

Aside from the question of morality, relativism is unable to answer the question of purpose. There are some who believe that the presence of human beings on the planet is the result of a random series of intermolecular mutations. If that is the case, from where or what did the idea of purpose arise?

Science is unable to explain or quantify beliefs like hope or faith. Nor can science explain the innate human pursuit of good, bad, right, wrong, fair play, equality or purpose. Our brains, according to evolutionists, developed through adaptation therefore leading us to discover and employ logic and logical thinking. This suggests that logic was a concept that existed before we could employ it. From where then did logic develop to be discovered? Where did logic come from? Where does good or right come from? What makes us to know when we are right or wrong? Science has no answers, only speculations that lead to more questions..

As mysterious as it seems, you and I have the ability to believe somehow and to comprehend that beyond the simplicity of our daily existence, lies a reason we are here. Have you ever asked yourself or wondered, 'Why am I here?' Have you ever asked the question, 'Is God real?' What about the question, "Where will I go when I die?"

For countless centuries, people have searched the annals of literature and philosophy to find the answers to these most basic yet profound human ponderings. Yet, for all the effort to find or invent answers, the truth lies in God's word. And, while there is something within all of humankind that resonates with the search for truth, it is only the discovery of truth that brings the assurance of peace with God, peace with ourselves and peace about our future.

The Bible tells us that God wants every person to be saved from the power and penalty of sin and to know the truth. For this reason, God has outlined in the Bible everything pertaining to life and godliness. *"This is good and pleases God our Savior, who wants everyone to be saved and to understand the truth"* (1Timothy 2:4).

The Sin Problem

How Did We Get Here?

"Yes, Adam's one sin brings condemnation for everyone, but Christ's one act of righteousness brings a right relationship with God and new life for everyone"
- The Apostle Paul

"In the beginning, God created the heavens and the earth" (Genesis 1:1*)*. As the scriptures continue, God created all life forms on the earth, including man and woman. From the beginning, it was God's plan to create a being God could love and with whom He could enjoy fellowship. God created man in His own image and likeness. That means God created man to be an intelligent living being, fully aware of himself and with authority over his environment and decisions.

Then God said, 'Let us make human beings in our image, to be like us. They will reign over the fish in the sea, the birds in the sky, the livestock, all the wild animals on the earth, and the small animals that scurry along the ground.' So God created human beings in his own image. In the image of God he created them; male and female he created them. Then God blessed them and said, 'Be fruitful and multiply. Fill the earth and govern it. Reign over the fish in the sea, the birds in the sky, and all the animals that scurry along the ground.' Then God said, 'Look! I have given you every seed-bearing plant throughout the earth and all the fruit trees for your food. And I have given every green plant as food for all the wild animals, the birds in the sky, and the small animals that scurry along the ground - everything that has life.' And that is what happened. Then God looked over all he had made, and he saw that it was very good! And evening passed and morning came, marking the sixth day (Genesis 1:26-31).

When God created Adam, God put Adam in the Garden of Eden to live. From the beginning, it was God's intention to provide a perfect environment for humankind complete with everything needed for life, and sustenance. God loved Adam and Eve so much that God even put a tree in the Garden called the Tree of Life from which human beings could eat continuously and live in their human bodies forever. The fruit on the Tree of Life was designed to fully nourish the human body.

Then the Lord God planted a garden in Eden in the east, and there he placed the man he had made. The Lord God made all sorts of trees grow up from the ground -

trees that were beautiful and that produced delicious fruit. In the middle of the garden he placed the tree of life and the Tree of the Knowledge of Good and Evil
(Genesis 2:8-9).

God created Adam and Eve to be free moral agents - that is to have free will and the ability to choose right or wrong. Some people question why God created humans with such decision making ability, but think of it this way. Is not love so much sweeter when people love you, honor you and spend time with you because they want to rather than out of obligation? God feels the same way. God wanted to create a being who, given the ability to decide, would choose to accept God's love and who would honor and love God wholeheartedly. For this reason, God put the Tree of the Knowledge of Good and Evil in the garden along with all of the other trees. God put the Tree of the Knowledge of Good and Evil in the garden to serve as a symbol of humankind's free will and choice of obedience.

You see, God instructed Adam to enjoy the fruit from all of the trees in the garden except for that of the Tree of the Knowledge of Good and Evil.

The Lord God placed the man in the Garden of Eden to tend and watch over it. But the Lord God warned him, 'You may freely eat the fruit of every tree in the garden - except the tree of the knowledge of

17

good and evil. If you eat its fruit, you are sure to die' (Genesis 2:15-17).

As long as Adam remained obedient to God, Adam enjoyed divine fellowship with God with a clear and undefiled conscience. Imagine that, though without clothes, Adam and Eve were perfectly comfortable and at ease in every way. *"Now the man and his wife were both naked, but they felt no shame"* (Genesis 2:25). From the beginning, neither death nor shame was ever a part of God's original plan for human beings. When Adam disobeyed God, he brought death upon himself and shame with it.

You may have read or heard the story of just how sin entered in and destroyed the perfect fellowship Adam and Eve had with God and each other.

The serpent was the shrewdest of all the wild animals the Lord God had made. One day he asked the woman, 'Did God really say you must not eat the fruit from any of the trees in the garden?' 'Of course we may eat fruit from the trees in the garden,' the woman replied. 'It's only the fruit from the tree in the middle of the garden that we are not allowed to eat. God said, 'You must not eat it or even touch it; if you do, you will die.'" 'You won't die!' the serpent replied to the woman. 'God knows that your eyes will be opened as soon as you eat it, and you will be like God, knowing both good and evil.' The woman was convinced. She saw that the tree was beautiful and its fruit looked delicious, and she wanted the wisdom it would give her. So she took some of the fruit and ate it. Then she gave some to her husband, who was with her, and he ate it, too. At that moment their eyes were opened, and they suddenly felt shame at their nakedness. So they sewed fig leaves together to cover themselves (Genesis 3:1-7).

Adam's disobedience caused the purity of his fellowship with God to be broken. Adam was tempted to doubt the word of God and gave in to that temptation willfully. Adam's act of willful disobedience induced consequences that would reverberate throughout the remaining generations of all of humankind. *"When Adam sinned, sin entered the world. Adam's sin brought death, so death spread to everyone, for everyone sinned"* (Romans 5:12). Adam utilized his free will for evil and not for good and in so doing, sinned against God through disobedience.

One could say that Adam basically turned away from what he knew was right in search of more. Adam decided that he wanted more than all God had provided. Adam wanted the supremacy that was beyond his station with God. The serpent had convinced Eve that she and Adam would, in a sense, become their own gods. Adam and Eve seized what they thought was the opportunity to live independently of God's authority over their lives.

The moment that Adam and Eve realized the magnitude of their actions, they hid themselves. They saw themselves and each other differently than before because now their souls were contaminated with the sin nature. Adam and Eve became what the Bible calls carnal. To be carnal means to be sensuous and ruled by the sinful nature of the flesh. Adam's one act of disobedience to God brought about the carnal nature that is innate in every human being. Because of Adam's sin, every succeeding generation has been born with the natural proclivity to be disobedient to God and rebel against God's authority.

Have you ever noticed a desire within you to be totally free from any rules and be answerable to no one? When satan deceived Eve, he did so by telling her that first, God's word was not true, and second, that she and Adam would be like God, knowing good and evil. Satan told Eve that she and Adam would not die as God had said but would instead become wise. Satan caused Eve to question the integrity of God's character and doubt the truth of God's word. The problem was that discovering good and evil disempowered Adam and Eve and made them slaves to sin because their discovery was birthed out of disobedience.

What neither Eve nor Adam thought about was that the Tree of Life God placed in the middle of the garden would have forever provided its fruit. The more Adam and Eve would eat of the tree of life, the longer they would live. But when Adam and Eve disobeyed, God not only disallowed them to eat anymore from the Tree of Life, but God removed Adam and Eve from the Garden of Eden altogether.

Then the Lord God said, 'Look, the human beings have become like us, knowing both good and evil. What if they reach out, take fruit from the tree of life, and eat it? Then they will live forever!' So the Lord God banished them from the Garden of Eden, and he sent Adam out to cultivate the ground from which he had been made (Genesis 3:23-24).

God was not going to allow Adam and Eve to continue to eat from the Tree of Life because Adam and Eve would live forever with a sin nature, making them prone to selfishness, rebellion and willful disobedience to God. Death came to Adam and Eve just as God said it would.

First, the sin nature replaced the God nature in Adam and Eve and sin brought about death. *"For the sin of this one man, Adam, brought death to many"* (Romans 5:15b). Second, when they could no longer eat from the Tree of Life, Adam and Eve's physical bodies decayed and they eventually died as has every person and generation since.

When Adam disobeyed God, both Adam and Eve realized that they had committed a horrible sin and they hid themselves as if they could hide from God. Have you ever tried to hide from God's all seeing eye? God called out to Adam and asked, *"Where are you?"* (Genesis 3:9).

God knew exactly where Adam and Eve were and what they had done. When God called out to Adam, God was really giving Adam something to think about. Adam had to ask himself, "Where am I?" The profundity of this simple question filled Adam with shame as the weight his sin began to descend upon him. Adam tells God that while he had heard God's voice in the garden, Adam was afraid because he was naked and so hid himself. One truth Adam expressed demonstrates his shame. *"I realized that I was naked"* (verse 10). God asked Adam another question, *"Who told you you were naked? Did you eat from the tree…?"* (verse 11).

Adam did as is typical of human beings ruled by the sin nature. Adam, rather than accept full responsibility for his decision to act out of self-interest rather than in accordance with God's instruction, blamed his wife. How often do we blame others when the responsibility of our decisions lies with us? Adam, in a roundabout way, blamed God actually. *"It was the woman you gave me who gave me the fruit, and I ate it."* (Genesis 3:12).

God spoke emphatically to Adam in Genesis 3:17-19.

> *And to the man he said, 'Since you listened to your wife and ate from the tree whose fruit I commanded you not to eat, the ground is cursed because of you. All your life you will struggle to scratch a living from it. It will grow thorns and thistles for you, though you will eat of its grains. By the sweat of your brow will you have food to eat until you return to the ground from which you were made. For you were made from dust, and to dust you will return.'*

God confronted satan, who had disguised himself as a serpent. God told the serpent that there would, from then on, be hatred between Eve's seed and that of the serpent. God further said that Eve's seed would bruise the head - that is to triumph over - the serpent's. *"And I will cause hostility between you and the woman and between your offspring and her offspring. He will strike your head and you will strike his heel"* (Genesis 3:15). When God made that promise, God was talking about Jesus and the victory that Jesus would exercise over Death and Hell through His sacrifice for humankind's salvation. (Genesis 3: 14-15).

Then the Lord God said to the serpent, 'Because you have done this, you are cursed more than all animals, domestic and wild. You will crawl on your belly, groveling in the dust as long as you live. And I will cause hostility between you and the woman, and between your offspring and her offspring. He will strike your head, and you will strike his heel.'

You see, when Adam disobeyed God, Adam broke fellowship with God for Adam and everyone who would be born after Adam. God is holy and sin cannot live in God's presence. That is why the scripture says that Adam's sin brought about death. *"When Adam sinned, sin entered the world. Adam's sin brought death, so death spread to everyone, for everyone sinned"* (Romans 5:12*)*. When Adam sinned through disobedience, he brought death upon all of humankind. God sending His Son, Jesus Christ, gave His life in obedience to God and freed humankind from the sentence of eternal death. Romans 6:23 tells us, *"For the wages of sin is death, but the free gift of God is eternal life through Christ Jesus our Lord."* Consider how God demonstrated His unconditional love for humankind.

But there is a great difference between Adam's sin and God's gracious gift. For the sin of this one man, Adam, brought death to many. But even greater is God's wonderful grace and his gift of forgiveness to many through this other man, Jesus Christ. And the result of God's gracious gift is very different from the result of that one man's sin. For Adam's sin led to condemnation, but God's free gift leads to our being made right with God, even though we are guilty of many sins. For the sin of this one man, Adam, caused death to rule over many. But even greater is God's wonderful grace and his gift of righteousness, for all who receive it will live in triumph over sin and death through this one man, Jesus Christ. Yes, Adam's one sin brings condemnation for everyone, but Christ's one act of righteousness brings a right relationship with God and new life for everyone. Because one person disobeyed God, many became sinners. But because one other person obeyed God, many will be made righteous (Romans 5:15-19).

Have you ever thought or made the statement, "I want to get right with God,' or 'I am going to get right with God?" Many people have. You are not alone in your desire to turn away from that which displeases God and violates His plans for your life.

In the flesh - that is on one's own - no one is able to live a life perfect enough to stand in the presence of complete holiness. No matter how hard we try, there will always be some thought or motivation or weakness or unintended sin we commit that separates us from complete and faultless fellowship with God.

Remember Adam and Eve? The serpent deceived Eve into believing that God's instruction and warning was just an attempt on God's part to keep the best part of life away from Eve and Adam. The serpent basically told Eve that God was only trying to keep her and Adam from being able to enjoy life more and to keep them restricted in their power, understanding and ability to make informed decisions for themselves knowing good from evil.

That is the same ploy satan uses today against well-intentioned people who struggle with obedience to God's word. Satan tells people, especially young people, that God does not want them to have fun and enjoy their youth. He tells young people that the life of a Christian, as outlined in the Bible, is too restrictive for the modern times in which we live. Far too often, people fall into traps that only serve to bring the same disappointments, consequences and shame Adam and Eve suffered when they believed the lie.

Adam was not deceived as Eve was, Adam consciously disobeyed. Adam's act of disobedience was Adam's way of acting out his independence as a living creature capable of logical thinking and reasoning. Adam was the one to whom God had given specific instructions and Adam knew firsthand what God said and meant. Satan, by deceiving Eve went around Adam as to not confront Adam directly. He figured that Eve would have more influence upon Adam. Through Eve, satan sought to awaken the desire within Adam to live his life his way and without constraint. That is, to be his own God, answerable to himself only. Adam became curious about that which heretofore belonged only to God. As much as God had provided in the garden for Adam and Eve, including perfect fellowship with God, Adam decided still to reach beyond the wisdom of the very God who created him. How have you reached beyond the wisdom of God in search of cosmic spiritual independence, that is spirituality without accountability?

What must Adam have been thinking about God for Adam to walk past all the vastness of God's free provision to reach for the one thing God instructed him, rather, commanded and warned Adam, to leave alone? God knew Adam's limitations. God knew that Adam would not be able to handle anything of the knowledge of good and evil.

Adam went from being a servant of God to a slave to sin because Adam decided in an instant to disobey - to become his own god. Because Adam knew better and made the conscious choice to disobey God, the consequences of Adam's sin affected the rest of humanity. When Adam decided to take his life into his own hands and turn away from the instructions that God had given him, Adam allowed satan to sow seeds of mistrust in what God had said. If Adam had maintained his trust in God, Adam would have resisted the temptation to doubt God's word. In spite of all that God had shown and given Adam, Adam decided to remove his trust from God and place it upon himself.

Unlike Eve's actions, Adam's caused the whole world to fall. From then on, no person on earth would enjoy unbroken fellowship with God or the pleasures of Eden. Willful disobedience hurt not only Adam, but all succeeding generations of people. Do you think it is possible that just before eating the forbidden fruit Adam thought to himself, 'It's my life, I am not hurting anyone!'

Look around you right now. Observe all that God has provided for you. Think about your family, your friends, your loved ones, your home, your health, your life. Sure, unlike the Garden of Eden, none may be perfect, but God has blessed you. If nothing else, God has given you the ability to read and understand this writing. Yet, in all the blessings God has provided there remains a void that only God can fill. Sometimes that void can only be filled with the knowledge that one has peace with God. If you were to be honest, can you admit that there might be some way that you can improve in your life to align better with God's will? Are you struggling with a desire that you know is not in accordance with God's desire for your life?

Because of Adam's disobedience to God, sin, shame and rebellion toward God became a part of humankind's nature from birth. Think about how easy it is to lie, think ungodly thoughts, be self-centered, entertain dishonest motives or to take unfair advantage of another person. To attempt to resist these inclinations presents a challenge that no human being can master all the time in every instance. In response to humankind's dilemma and ongoing struggle with right and wrong, we say, 'Nobody's perfect.' That is true, no one is perfect, but God is. God is perfect in every way. How then can a person decide to get right with God who is perfect?

Who Is Jesus and Why Do I Need Him?

"Without question, this is the great mystery of our faith : Christ was revealed in a human body and vindicated by the Spirit. He was seen by angels and announced to the nations. He was believed in throughout the world and taken to heaven in glory."

- I Timothy 3:16

"The law of Moses was unable to save us because of the weakness of or sinful nature. So God did what the law could not do. He sent his own Son in a body like the bodies we sinners have. And in that body God declared an end to sin's control over us by giving his Son as a sacrifice for our sins."

- Romans 8:3

You may remember hearing or learning about the Ten Commandments, also known as *The Law*. God originally gave the Ten Commandments to Moses so that the people would understand their inability to keep them. God knew that human beings, once tainted with the sin nature brought upon all humanity through Adam, would not be able live sinless lives. And, God intended to send His Son, Jesus, to redeem humankind all along.

Remember, in the Garden of Eden, God told satan that the seed of the woman would bruise the head of satan. God had the plan of salvation for humankind before Adam sinned because God knew Adam would disobey. In the interim, however, God needed to let human beings see for themselves their need for a savior. Adam demonstrated in the Garden of Eden that God's commandment was not enough to dissuade him. Adam, who had to see for himself, passed the appetite for sin and the propensity to second-guess God on to the rest of humanity.

For centuries, people of all nations and creeds tried to keep the Ten Commandments and the subsequent rules for worship and piety and failed. The priests, in ancient days, used to present sacrifices, pray and ask forgiveness for humankind's sin. This was an elaborate and sacred undertaking because of all the requirements involved. Still, for hundreds of years people tried and could not keep what became known as *The Law*. People had to get to a place where they understood that *The Law* - that is the knowledge of sin - prevented people from full fellowship with God.

In the centuries between *The Law* and the birth of Jesus, people struggled and failed in their attempts to achieve righteousness before God. The best human beings could hope for was God's acceptance of their individual attempts at piety and goodness in keeping of *The Law*.

God's law was given so that all people could see how sinful they were. But as people sinned more and more, God's wonderful grace became more abundant. So just as sin ruled over all people and brought them to death, now God's wonderful grace rules instead, giving us right standing with God and resulting in eternal life through Jesus Christ our Lord (Romans 5:20-21).

When Adam sinned, Adam caused separation in humanity's relationship with God. God sent His Son, Jesus, because God want's that relationship back. Merely paying homage to God through sacrifices in the days of antiquity before Jesus was insufficient to restore relationship. God provided salvation through His Son, Jesus Christ, as *the way* to reconcile human beings to Himself and once again provide the full fellowship with God Adam forfeited for sin. God, from the beginning, created human beings for fellowship. God wants a relationship with you and me. He does not want to be known as some far away judge sitting on a throne in heaven watching and waiting to punish people for sinning.

God wanted relationship with us when He created Adam and He wants relationship today. Jesus was the perfect sacrifice, which is why His death is sufficient to restore all of humanity to right relationship with God. The sacrifices of old were imperfect and could not bear the weight of humankind's sin. But Jesus, who lived a perfectly sinless life, paid the penalty for your sin and mine and restored us to the place of being able to have full fellowship and relationship with God. Because of Jesus' sacrifice, you and I do not have to strive to keep *The Law*. Romans 8:1-4 assures us.

> *So now there is no condemnation for those who belong to Christ Jesus. And because you belong to him, the power of the life-giving Spirit has freed you from the power of sin that leads to death. The law of Moses was unable to save us because of the weakness of our sinful nature. So God did what the law could not do. He sent his own Son in a body like the bodies we sinners have. And in that body God declared an end to sin's control over us by giving his Son as a sacrifice for our sins. He did this so that the just requirement of the law would be fully satisfied for us, who no longer follow our sinful nature but instead follow the Spirit.*

Romans 6:23 assures us. *"For the wages of sin is death, but the free gift of God is eternal life through Christ Jesus our Lord."* Sin brought about death. Our sin, yours, mine and that of all humanity brought about death, but instead of us having to die for our own sin individually, Jesus died for us. Jesus, who was innocent in living a sinless life, died so that you and I, the guilty, could go free.

When we were utterly helpless, Christ came at just the right time and died for us sinners. Now, most people would not be willing to die for an upright person, though someone might perhaps be willing to die for a person who is especially good. But God showed his great love for us by sending Christ to die for us while we were still sinners. And since we have been made right in God's sight by the blood of Christ, he will certainly save us from God's condemnation. For since our friendship with God was restored by the death of his Son while we were still his enemies, we will certainly be saved through the life of his Son. So now we can rejoice in our wonderful new relationship with God because our Lord Jesus Christ has made us friends of God (Romans 5:6-11).

And this is the love of which I write in beginning this text. God's love for you is so strong that He would rather die on a cross than live in all the splendor of heaven without you. He would rather die than not have a personal relationship with you.

You have probably been misunderstood in your life at times, even when you had good intentions. Jesus knows how you feel. The most misunderstood and controversial person in all of earth's history and creation is Jesus Christ. Jesus' whole purpose in coming to earth and dying on the cross of Calvary was to redeem humankind from the power and penalty of sin and, in this way, restore fellowship between God and man. *"For if, when we were enemies, we were reconciled to God by the death of his Son, much more, being reconciled, we shall be saved by his life"* (Romans 5:10, King James Version, KJV).

As simple as it may sound, there was nothing simple about it. Jesus suffered and died a horrible, agonizingly dreadful and violent death. He subjected Himself to the shame imposed upon Him for our sin. You see, the price of sin had to be paid in blood. Jesus gave His blood so you and I do not have to. Without the shedding of blood, the Bible says, there is no remittance of sin. *"In fact, according to the law of Moses, nearly everything was purified with blood. For without the shedding of blood, there is no forgiveness"* (Hebrews 9:22). God loved the world so much that He sent His Son, Jesus, to die once and for all.

> *For Christ did not enter into a holy place made with human hands, which was only a copy of the true one in heaven. He entered into heaven itself to appear now before God on our behalf. And he did not enter heaven to offer himself again and again, like the high priest here on earth who enters the Most Holy Place year after year with the blood of an animal. If that had been necessary, Christ would have had to die*

again and again, ever since the world began. But now, once for all time, he has appeared at the end of the age to remove sin by his own death as a sacrifice. (Hebrews 9:24-26).

Beloved, understand this. It is God's desire to move beyond the sin problem. That is the reason He sent His Son, Jesus. Before Jesus, man's whole preoccupation when it came to being right before God was the issue of sin. Jesus came to defeat sin in the flesh for us so that we could get on with the business of relating to our God the way God intended from the beginning with Adam.

The law of Moses was unable to save us because of the weakness of our sinful nature. So God did what the law could not do. He sent his own Son in a body like the bodies we sinners have. And in that body God declared an end to sin's control over us by giving his Son as a sacrifice for our sins. He did this so that the just requirement of the law would be fully satisfied for us, who no longer follow our sinful nature but instead follow the Spirit (Romans 8:3-4).

Before Adam sinned, Adam had a close relationship with God. But after his disobedience, Adam hid from God and humankind has been hiding from God ever since. *"When the cool evening breezes were blowing, the man and his wife heard the LORD God walking about in the garden. So they hid from the LORD God among the trees. Then the LORD God called to the man, 'Where are you?'"* (Genesis 3:8-9).

God called out to Adam when Adam was hiding and God is calling out to people today through His Son, Jesus Christ. There is no need to hide, no need to be afraid. God is looking for you and calling out to you. You hear Him calling in your heart. God is not calling out for you because He does not know where you are. God is calling out for *you* to understand and realize where you are. You occupy a special place within the heart of God reserved just for you. You mean the world to him. In dying on the cross for you, God proves you mean more than life to Him.

You may ask, "What about the awful sins I have committed?" There is no sin for which Jesus did not give His life. There is no sin more dreadful than rejecting Jesus' sacrifice. People who reject Jesus' sacrifice die to pay their own price for their sins. They die an unnecessary sinner's death and spend eternity out of fellowship with God. Human reasoning may suggest that no such sacrifice could exist.

Secular humanism suggests that all truth is relative so that what is true for one person may not be true for another. But the Bible is clear when it comes to understanding truth. When challenged by

Thomas, *"Jesus told him, "I am the way, the truth, and the life. No one can come to the Father except through me"* (John 14:6).

There is no way to go around Jesus to get to God. And, all roads do not lead to the same god. *"Ye are my witnesses, saith the LORD, and my servant whom I have chosen: that ye may know and believe me, and understand that I am he: before me there was no God formed, neither shall there be after me. I, even I, am the LORD; and beside me there is no Saviour"* (Isaiah 43:10-11, KJV).

The divinity of Jesus cannot be denied. *"And without controversy great is the mystery of godliness: God was manifest in the flesh, justified in the Spirit, seen of angels, preached unto the Gentiles, believed on in the world, received up into glory."* (I Timothy 3:16, KJV). Jesus is God. Consider the gospel of John.

> *In the beginning the Word already existed. The Word was with God, and the Word was God. He existed in the beginning with God. God created everything through him, and nothing was created except through him. The Word gave life to everything that was created, and his life brought light to everyone. The light shines in the darkness, and the darkness can never extinguish it* (verses 1-5).

39

When God created human beings, God was talking to the Word who was with God and who was God. *"Then God said, "Let us make human beings in our image, to be like us" (Genesis* 1:26). John sheds further light on the Word. *"So the Word became human and made his home among us. He was full of unfailing love and faithfulness. And we have seen his glory, the glory of the Father's one and only Son"* (John 1:14). Psalm 46:10 tells us, *"Be still, and know that I am God! I will be honored by every nation. I will be honored throughout the world."*

Take no chances with your soul, Beloved. Jesus loves you and He died so you can live in all the fullness and joy that God has in store for you. This life, however joyous or difficult it has been is all the hell you will ever know. But, for those who reject Christ, this life is all the heaven they will ever know.

Take no chances with your soul. Put not your faith in the words of men and women who reason and rationalize God out of creation and Jesus out of salvation.

As learned as those scholars may be, not one was here when the world was formed. When they knew themselves they were here on this earth with the ability to think and interact just like you, I and every other human being.

Here is wisdom. At the heart of the resistance to God and especially the atoning blood of Jesus Christ is the desire to live without being accountable to anyone. You see, to acknowledge God and accept His love means recognizing His desire that we demonstrate our love and appreciation for His sacrifice. Sure, Jesus died for our sins and accepting Jesus' sacrifice means our sins are forgiven, but that does not give license to sin willingly and knowingly without conscience. *"Well then, should we keep on sinning so that God can show us more and more of his wonderful grace? Of course not! Since we have died to sin, how can we continue to live in it?"* (Romans 6:1-2). Moreover, does not the mere realization of what Jesus did for you bring joy and gratefulness to your heart?

Beloved, it is no coincidence that you are reading this right now. God loves you and has been watching over you and protecting you and providing for you your whole life. God has brought you to this exact moment in time to minister to your heart again. This is not His first attempt to help you understand His love for you. You have been looking for love your entire life and God has been right here all the time. The love of human beings is limited and often comes with conditions, and that is no one's fault really because the sin-nature that Adam caused to come upon all human beings placed limitations on all our abilities to love unconditionally. That is the reason we question God when we do not understand life or when things have not gone as planned. God understands that. Psalm 103:14 tells us, *"The LORD is like a father to his children, tender and compassionate to those who fear him. For he knows how weak we are; he remembers we are only dust."*

There is a saying in the world that to know someone is to love that person. Well, to know God is to love Him. God knows us and He loves us anyway.

There is nothing you have done or will do now or in the future to erase or lessen God's love for you. There is no sin that Jesus did not atone for with His precious blood. Nothing can separate you from the love that God has for you - nothing and nobody.

Can anything ever separate us from Christ's love? Does it mean he no longer loves us if we have trouble or calamity, or are persecuted, or hungry, or destitute, or in danger, or threatened with death? (As the Scriptures say, 'For your sake we are killed every day; we are being slaughtered like sheep.') No, despite all these things, overwhelming victory is ours through Christ, who loved us. And I am convinced that nothing can ever separate us from God's love. Neither death nor life, neither angels nor demons, neither our fears for today nor our worries about tomorrow—not even the powers of hell can separate us from God's love. No power in the sky above or in the earth below—indeed, nothing in all creation will ever be able to separate us from the love of God that is revealed in Christ Jesus our Lord (Romans 8:35-39).

Won't you accept Jesus into your heart today? There is no preparation needed. You do not have to try to change anything about your life first. That is a lie the devil tells people in order to get people to procrastinate and put it off for another day.

Jesus does not require anything but your made up mind to accept His sacrifice for your sins. Jesus died for all sin, past, present and future. How can I say future? Because, you and I had not been born when Jesus died, yet His blood was shed for us. We were in the future. You do not have to try to stop sinning before you accept Christ.

Remember *The Law*? The Bible let us know, as we discussed previously, that Jesus' sacrifice for our sins set us free from *The Law*. We are redeemed from trying to earn God's love and acceptance. Because Jesus died for us, we do not have to die for our sin. Jesus' death for us earned our way into heaven, not our good works. You may be a good person and the good you have done will not go unnoticed by God. God will reward His children on earth and in heaven, but one has to get to heaven in order to be rewarded. The only way to get to heaven is to receive Jesus Christ as Savior and Lord. It is only the shed blood of Jesus that atones for our sin.

While you may indeed be a very good person, can you truthfully say you have never sinned? No. None of us can. That is the reason Jesus died, because it is impossible for any human being to live a totally sinless life. When we accept Jesus, we are saved by His grace.

> Grace is not earned or merited. Grace just is. *"God saved you by his grace when you believed. And you can't take credit for this; it is a gift from God. Salvation is not a reward for the good things we have done, so none of us can boast about it. For we are God's masterpiece. He has created us anew in Christ Jesus, so we can do the good things he planned for us long ago"* (Ephesians 2:8-10).

Consider Romans 8:4, 9-10.

> *For Christ has already accomplished the purpose for which the law was given. As a result, all who believe in him are made right with God. [...] If you openly declare that Jesus is Lord and believe in your heart that God raised him from the dead, you will be saved. For it is by believing in your heart that you are made right with God, and it is by openly declaring your faith that you are saved.*

Beloved, believe in your heart and pray this prayer with me.

Dear Lord Jesus, I acknowledge that I have sinned and fallen short of the glory of God. I repent for my sins and denounce my sin and all the works of satan in my life. I thank you for shedding your precious blood on the cross for the remission of my sins and I receive your sacrifice for me now. I believe that you died for me and that you were raised from the dead. Lord Jesus, come into my heart right now. Be my Savior and Lord, Redeemer and friend. Fill me with the precious Holy Spirit. In your name, Jesus Christ, I pray. Amen.

Beloved, if you believe in your heart as the scriptures say, you are saved. You have been forgiven for your sins and they are now washed away. You no longer have to live in guilt or shame for anything you have done in the past. If you sin again, you will not lose your salvation. You are today a child of God and nothing, not even sin, can separate you from His love which has redeemed you. You did not cause or earn your salvation by being good, so you cannot lose your salvation by being bad. Remember, Jesus paid the price for your salvation. Do not allow old memories, weaknesses, people or satan to torment you. You are saved and today begins the best of the rest of your life. Jesus will now begin the work of helping you to become your best self with the help of the Holy Spirit.

The Holy Spirit is, in essence, Jesus living inside of your heart helping you, guiding you, teaching you and giving you understanding of His love and purpose for your life. God created you with a specific purpose and will now begin to lead you toward that purpose.

When you feel the urge to pray, *that is Jesus.* Listen. When you feel the urge to read your Bible, listen. *That is Jesus.* When you feel the urge to forgive and ask others for forgiveness. *That is Jesus* working within you to bring you into His purpose for your life. Jesus wants you to live free of heavy burdens of shame and guilt. While we may have repented for our sin before God, it may sometimes be necessary to ask forgiveness of someone we have wronged in order to free that person from the pain we may have caused.

> *Then Jesus said, "Come to me, all of you who are weary and carry heavy burdens, and I will give you rest. Take my yoke upon you. Let me teach you, because I am humble and gentle at heart, and you will find rest for your souls. For my yoke is easy to bear, and the burden I give you is light*
> (Matthew 1:29-30).

It is important, Beloved, to pray and ask God to lead you to a Bible teaching church so that you can learn of your Savior, participate in worship services and fellowship with other Christians. You have a bright future in Christ.

Your New Life in Christ

*"And let us not neglect our meeting together,
as some people do, but encourage one another,
especially now that the day of his return is drawing
near."*

- Hebrews 10:25

Choosing a Church Home

As a new Christian, it is important for you to take the time to sit and learn. You cannot teach yourself. Hebrews 10:25 is very clear. *"And let us not neglect our meeting together, as some people do, but encourage one another, especially now that the day of his return is drawing near."* It is deception to think you do not need a pastor or church family to help cultivate your growth in Christ. Thoughts like this come to lull you into isolation, which is dangerous, especially for a new Christian. This is the way of confusion. It is vitally important for you to attend a Bible believing church where you can learn the word of God regularly.

You have probably noticed countless churches all around you. Perhaps you have visited a few of them. There are many, many Christians all over the

49

world and you can likely find a good church home wherever you are.

How do you know when you find the church and pastor that are right for you? First, you will hear the Bible being preached in its fullness. That is, you will hear preaching that Biblically based. God is the creator and sustainer of all life (Genesis 1:1). Jesus Christ is God's only begotten Son who died on the cross of Calvary for the sins of the world (John 3:16). Jesus lived a completely sinless life and after dying on the cross for the world's sins, rose from the dead by the Spirit of God and ascended into Heaven where He sits at the right hand of the Father, interceding for us and is alive for evermore.

Who is the Holy Spirit?

The Holy Spirit is the Spirit of Jesus who lives inside the heart of Christians to bring truth. The Holy Spirit is alive and helps Christians to pray, understand God's word and worship Jesus. The Holy Spirit brings healing and works miracles. The Holy Spirit leads and guides Christians into all truth. He convicts Christians of sin, but does not condemn.

When we are wrong, the Holy Spirit lets us know in order to bring correction through His love. The Holy Spirit will point out a sinful action or wrong decision without condemning you as a bad person. Condemnation brings rejection. The Holy Spirit rejects sin but will never reject you. He will always love you, want you near Him and hear your cry. Try not to grieve the Holy Spirit. You can grieve the Holy Spirit – that is offend Him or make Him unwelcome. A few of the ways we grieve the Holy Spirit include, doubting Him or His love for us, disobeying God's word, willful sin, causing pain to others, worshipping something or someone other than the Lord, Jesus Christ and mixing the gospel of Jesus Christ with Spiritism, mysticism, relativism, secular humanism or other erroneous teachings.

The Bible believing church God has for you will have Bible study in addition to worship services. Attend Bible study regularly. Bible study is dedicated to learning God's word, learning about Jesus and educating you about your place in Him. In Bible study you will often be able to ask questions and participate in Bible discussions that help you see yourself in God's plan. Many large churches will have small group programs in addition to the church wide Bible study services. Stay away from any study groups not sanctioned by your church.

The reason it is important to allow the Holy Spirit to lead you to the church He has for you is because it is in this church that you will grow and learn. In the church the Holy Spirit leads you to, the worship will satisfy your spirit and the preached word will minister directly to you. The pastor God has for you will preach and teach God's word in such a way that speaks to your heart as if you are hearing a word from God especially for you. You will go in hungry and leave fulfilled having received a full word (called a Rhema word) from God. The pastor God has for you will be used by God to cultivate your spiritual growth and preparation. You will begin to see yourself evolving and maturing in Christ and in your understanding of God's word. Your pastor will be someone you can trust and who will help you understand through God's word your significance as a Christian.

In the church God has for you, you will find fellowship with other Christians and a place for you to serve. As you begin to grow in your relationship with Jesus, begin to get involved in your church. God has given you unique gifts and talents that are designed to help build the ministry. Becoming involved in the church keeps you connected and accountable and helps you to grow in your relationships with Christ and with others.

Any church in which the deity of Jesus Christ is not taught is not a Bible believing church. If you find yourself in the midst of erroneous teachings about Jesus being only a prophet and not God, leave quickly and do not look back. Any place where a human being or someone other than Jesus Christ receives worship is not of God. Leave quickly and do not look back. All roads **do not** lead to heaven. All roads **do not** lead to God. Be not deceived. Jesus Christ is not merely one of the many ways to

reach God or heaven. Jesus is God. Consider I
Timothy 3:16

> *Without question, this is the great mystery
> of our faith: Christ was revealed in a
> human body and vindicated by the Spirit.
> He was seen by angels and announced to
> the nations. He was believed in throughout
> the world and taken to heaven in glory.*

John 14:6 tell us as… *"Jesus told him, 'I am the
way, the truth, and the life. No one can come to the
Father except through me.'"*

We do not know everything there is to know
about God or His ways, but we know that His word
says that Jesus is the way. We also know that it is
God's will that the whole world learn of Him. II
Peter 3:9 tells us that Jesus wants no one to be lost.
*"The Lord isn't really being slow about his promise,
as some people think. No, he is being patient for
your sake. He does not want anyone to be destroyed,
but wants everyone to repent."* This is why Jesus
wants Christians to share their faith with others.
*"And then he told them, "Go into all the world and
preach the Good News to everyone. Anyone who
believes and is baptized will be saved. But anyone
who refuses to believe will be condemned."* (Mark
16:15-16).

Once you establish a Bible believing church
home, it is important for you to be baptized. Jesus

was baptized by John the Baptist. *"One day when the crowds were being baptized, Jesus himself was baptized. As he was praying, the heavens opened,"* (Luke 3:21).

Baptism signifies dying to the sinful nature and rising to live in Christ. When we are baptized, we are submerged into a watery grave symbolically and we rise as a new creature. As Jesus rose from the dead, so we rise from being dead in our sin to being alive in Christ. *"For we died and were buried with Christ by baptism. And just as Christ was raised from the dead by the glorious power of the Father, now we also may live new lives"* (Romans 6:4). On the day of Pentecost, Jesus' disciples began preaching the Gospel of Jesus Christ. *"Peter replied, "Each of you must repent of your sins and turn to God, and be baptized in the name of Jesus Christ for the forgiveness of your sins. Then you will receive the gift of the Holy Spirit"* (Acts 2:38).

Ask God to fill you with the Holy Spirit. Jesus promised that the Holy Spirit whom you received to be with you when you accepted Jesus in your heart would come and live within you. *"And I will ask the Father, and he will give you another Advocate, who will never leave you. He is the Holy Spirit, who leads into all truth. The world cannot receive him, because it isn't looking for him and doesn't recognize him. But you know him, because he lives with you now and later will be in you"* (John 14:16-17). Read also about the first Christians who received the Holy

Spirit in Acts 2. Some call this the baptism or filling of the Holy Spirit.

> *On the day of Pentecost all the believers were meeting together in one place. Suddenly, there was a sound from heaven like the roaring of a mighty windstorm, and it filled the house where they were sitting. Then, what looked like flames or tongues of fire appeared and settled on each of them. And everyone present was filled with the Holy Spirit and began speaking in other languages, as the Holy Spirit gave them this ability* (Acts 2:1-4).

The Holy Spirit is Jesus living inside of you to lead and guide you and give you understanding of God's word. The Holy Spirit also heals people. Jesus healed people by the power of the Holy Spirit. *"And you know that God anointed Jesus of Nazareth with the Holy Spirit and with power. Then Jesus went around doing good and healing all who were oppressed by the devil, for God was with him"* (Acts 10:38).

In addition to giving you direction and insight into God's word for your life, the Holy Spirit will empower you to share your faith and to be a conduit through which He performs miracles for you and through you for others. Jesus told his disciples that they would receive power upon being filled with the Holy Spirit. This promise is for all Christians, including you. *"But you will receive power when the Holy Spirit comes upon you. And you will be my witnesses, telling people about me everywhere - in Jerusalem, throughout Judea, in Samaria, and to the ends of the earth"*(Acts 1:8).

Begin to share your faith with other people. Tell other people about Jesus, but avoid arguments and debates. As a new Christian, it is important for you to learn and solidify your faith before engaging in tumultuous debates Leave folks who want to argue or denounce Christ to a more seasoned Christian and resolve simply to pray for them. The Scriptures remind us. *"[…] Guard what God has entrusted to you. Avoid godless, foolish discussions with those who oppose you with their so-called knowledge. Some people have wandered from the faith by following such foolishness"* (1Timothy 6:20).

Trials, Tribulations and Temptations

"For we walk by faith, not by sight:"

- II Corinthians 5:7

When the trials of life become difficult, hold on to your faith and believe Jesus above all. Trials may be described as circumstances or events that arise to challenge your faith. Trials often represent a period of grievous and sometimes prolonged difficulty in one or more areas of life. Satan, and sometimes people, may try to convince you that your circumstances, which may appear to contradict the promises of God at times, suggest that God does not exist, is not faithful or does not really love you.

During a trial, your faith, while tested, grows when you persevere. God's purpose in allowing trials is to help us learn to resist the natural inclination to give up and give in to fear, doubt, worry or unbelief. One of the major lessons we learn in our Christian walk is to trust God when we cannot see Him. Through trials we learn to sit in our resolve, that is to stubbornly hold on to our faith and trust God's heart toward us, especially when we cannot see His hand moving for us.

Tribulations are similar to trials in that your faith is tested in both. However, tribulations are often prolonged periods of anguish, afflictions, distresses and vexations of soul caused by great suffering. Tribulations may arise out of some element of persecution or life choice that defers to God's will over one's own.

Temptations are enticements that come to get us to give in to sinful desires or inclinations. While God may allow circumstances to test your faith, God will never tempt you to sin. Temptation comes from satan and our own desires for the things of the flesh. Temptations reveal ourselves to us. When we are tempted, we come face to face with our own flaws and propensities. Temptations reveal to us the areas we need God to minister to within us. Temptations do not come from God, temptations come from within.

> *And remember, when you are being tempted, do not say, "God is tempting me." God is never tempted to do wrong, and he never tempts anyone else. Temptation comes from our own desires, which entice us and drag us away. These desires give birth to sinful actions. And when sin is allowed to grow, it gives birth to death. So don't be misled, my dear brothers and sisters. Whatever is good and perfect is a gift coming down to us from God our Father, who created all the lights in the*

heavens. He never changes or casts a shifting shadow (James 1:13-17).

The good news about temptations is that God is present and with you to help you withstand. You may have heard people misquote the Bible in stating that God will never put on you more than you can bear. Again, beloved, God does not put temptation upon anyone. God cannot be tempted by sin, nor does He tempt us to sin. The correct meaning behind the misunderstood Scripture verse is that you and I are never left alone to deal with temptations, especially temptations that could overwhelm us.

The temptations in your life are no different from what others experience. And God is faithful. He will not allow the temptation to be more than you can stand. When you are tempted, he will show you a way out so that you can endure (I Corinthians 10:13).

God is there with us and creates a way out every time. It is up to us, beloved, when faced with the choice to give in to the temptation or take the way out, to acknowledge the escape God is providing and take it without hesitation.

You may have heard of the young man, Joseph, in the Bible who was faced with the temptation of giving in to his manager's wife who wanted to sleep with him. Joseph had been through tremendous persecution in his life at the hands of his brothers, and a time came when Joseph thought his life was taking a positive turn. He had a new job working for one of the Egypt's political leaders. Joseph enjoyed great favor from his manager who entrusted Joseph more than anyone. One day, while Joseph's manager was away, his manager's wife approached Joseph.

Joseph was a young man and obviously perceived by his manager's wife as virile and strong. Joseph, when faced with the temptation to sleep with another man's wife and betray his manager's trust chose to acknowledge and take the way of escape God provided for him. Joseph ran away.

Joseph did not try to reason with his manager's wife any more after refusing her almost daily. The woman tried to grab Joseph's jacket to make him stay and rather than use that as an excuse to give in, Joseph ran out of his jacket and left it there with her. Unfortunately, this incident would cause Joseph to endure a tribulation caused by persecution. When Joseph's manager returned home, his wife lied on Joseph and told her husband that Joseph had tried to molest her. Joseph's manager then fired Joseph from his job and put Joseph in jail. Joseph had done what was right and suffered for it – this was tribulation in action.

Joseph was a very handsome and well-built young man, and Potiphar's wife soon began to look at him lustfully. "Come and sleep with me," she demanded. But Joseph refused. "Look," he told her, "my master trusts me with everything in his entire household. No one here has more authority than I do. He has held back nothing from me except you, because you are his wife. How could I do such a wicked thing? It would be a great sin against God."

She kept putting pressure on Joseph day after day, but he refused to sleep with her, and he kept out of her way as much as possible. One day, however, no one else was around when he went in to do his work. She came and grabbed him by his cloak, demanding, "Come on, sleep with me!" Joseph tore himself away, but he left his cloak in her hand as he ran from the house.

When she saw that she was holding his cloak and he had fled, she called out to her servants. Soon all the men came running. "Look!" she said. "My husband has brought this Hebrew slave here to make fools of us! He came into my room to rape me, but I screamed. When he heard me scream, he ran outside and got away, but he left his cloak behind with me."

She kept the cloak with her until her husband came home. Then she told him her story. "That Hebrew slave you've brought into our house tried to come in and fool

*around with me," she said. "But when I
screamed, he ran outside, leaving his cloak
with me!" Potiphar was furious when he
heard his wife's story about how Joseph
had treated her. So he took Joseph and
threw him into the prison where the king's
prisoners were held, and there he remained*
(Genesis 39:6b-20).

God is faithful, however, even in tribulation.
God was with Joseph during Joseph's tribulation and
God used that time to develop Joseph's character and
prepare Joseph for the destiny God had planned for
Joseph all along. Through all of Josephs trials,
temptations and tribulations, God prepared Joseph to
rule over all of Egypt and secure prosperity for his
people. This could not be accomplished without
Joseph's heart being in the right place. God had to
make and mold Joseph into the leader of great
historical significance God destined Joseph to be.
Jesus, the Savior of the world, would descend
through the lineage of Joseph.

You see, beloved, God's priorities for us are not
always in line with our priorities for ourselves. It is
during periods of trials, temptations and tribulations
that we come face to face with the conflicts within
us. God's goal in each of our lives is to make us
become the highest and best form of ourselves.
God's goal is to clean us up and make us people of
character, of integrity and of humility and love –
children of God so much so that in any given

situation we behave just like our Heavenly Father. Real and authentic power with God begins with exercising power over self and self-will.

The Apostle Luke explains how the Holy Spirit led Jesus into the wilderness to be tempted by the devil. The Bible tell us that Jesus was full of the Holy Spirit when He went into the wilderness, but after enduring the temptations by the devil victoriously, Jesus returned with *power* - the *power* of the Holy Spirit.

> *Then Jesus, full of the Holy Spirit, returned from the Jordan River. He was led by the Spirit in the wilderness,[where he was tempted by the devil for forty days. Jesus ate nothing all that time and became very hungry [...] Then Jesus returned to Galilee, filled with the Holy Spirit's power* (Luke 4:1-2,14).

You may have heard of Job. Job said, in the midst of his trials, *"...all the days of my appointed time will I wait, till my change come"* (Job 14:14). As Christians, we learn to live by believing and not by seeing. *"For we live by believing and not by seeing"* (II Corinthians 5:7). We learn to trust God when we cannot trust anyone else or even ourselves. God tells us in His word that His thoughts are not our thoughts. Neither are His ways our ways.

For just as the heavens are higher than the earth, so my ways are higher than your ways and my thoughts higher than your thoughts. The rain and snow come down from the heavens and stay on the ground to water the earth. They cause the grain to grow, producing seed for the farmer and bread for the hungry. It is the same with my word. I send it out, and it always produces fruit. It will accomplish all I want it to, and it will prosper everywhere I send it (Isaiah 55:9-11).

Commit this verse to memory. *"This is the confidence we have in approaching God: that if we ask anything according to his will, he hears us. And if we know that he hears us - whatever we ask - we know that we have what we asked of him"* (1 John 5:14-15).

How can you know what God's will is? You can know by reading and studying His word, the Bible. Healing is God's will. Jesus said, *"The Spirit of the Lord is upon me, for he has anointed me to bring Good News to the poor. He has sent me to proclaim that captives will be released, that the blind will see, that the oppressed will be set free, and that the time of the Lord's favor has come"* (Luke 4:18). 1 Peter 2:24 assures us. *"He [Jesus] personally carried our sins in his body on the cross so that we can be dead to sin and live for what is right. By his wounds   you are healed."*

Provision is God's will. *"And this same God who takes care of me will supply all your needs from his glorious riches, which have been given to us in Christ Jesus"* (Philippians 4:19).

For you to have peace, guidance and direction in your life is God's will. *"Don't worry about anything; instead, pray about everything. Tell God what you need, and thank him for all he has done. Then you will experience God's peace, which exceeds anything we can understand. His peace will guard your hearts and minds as you live in Christ Jesus"* (Philippians 4:6-7). Proverbs 3:5-6 instructs us. *"Trust in the Lord with all your heart; do not depend on your own understanding. Seek his will in all you do, and he will show you which path to take."*

It is God's will for the lonely to have a family *"God places the lonely in families; he sets the prisoners free and gives them joy"* (Psalm 68:6). *"Then the Lord God said, 'It is not good for the man to be alone. I will make a helper who is just right for him'"* (Genesis 2:19).

Yes, God has so many promises in His word for you and they are all His will. When you pray, talk to God about His word. Speak God's word and promises over yourself and over your life and future. Resist every temptation to speak contrary to what God's word says about you or any circumstance in your life, including your health or family.

Then Jesus said to the disciples, "Have faith in God. I tell you the truth, you can say to this mountain, 'May you be lifted up and thrown into the sea,' and it will happen. But you must really believe it will happen and have no doubt in your heart. I tell you, you can pray for anything, and if you believe that you've received it, it will be yours. But when you are praying, first forgive anyone you are holding a grudge against, so that your Father in heaven will forgive your sins, too (Mark 11:22-26).

Forgiveness is vitally important in the life of a Christian. It can be one of the most challenging mandates Jesus has given us, but He did so for many reasons. Primarily, it is God's will for you and I to be like Jesus. Jesus not only forgave those who persecuted Him, but asked the Father in heaven to forgive them also. When we forgive, we give up our right to hold peoples' wrong against them. You may not feel like forgiving. You may not feel as if you have forgiven, but you can make a decision to let go of the anger, resentment or bitterness in your heart toward someone. It may not be easy, but the Holy Spirit can help you.

Recently, I called a state motor vehicle office in an attempt to help someone reconcile a ten year old traffic violation. This friend had become ill some years ago and the illness had actually been the cause of the traffic violation. As I attempted to explain the circumstances of the traffic violation, I noticed that, while politely listening, the agent represented an unforgiving institution. The agency had held on to its right to impose a fine for nearly ten years. And when I visited the web-site to learn how to facilitate a medical exception, I found none. The verbiage on the web-site clearly stated that the agency would hold on to the right to impose fines forever! This is exactly how unforgiveness works. Unforgiveness holds on to its right to make one pay for one's offense and refuses to let go. There are some offenses, like my friend's traffic ticket, that are not worth holding on to. There are offenses, however, that are life altering and deeply damaging to one's well-being. These are far more difficult to forgive because the injured party is often left with the fragmented pieces of a life once whole. In cases like this, the Holy Spirit is the only One who can help bring about a forgiving heart.

This is one of the major benefits of being filled with the Holy Spirit. The Holy Spirit comes to live with you when you receive Christ, but when you have the experience of being filled with the Holy Spirit, or, as some call it receiving the baptism of the Holy Spirit, He lives inside of you and gives you grace.

A Word About Faith

One day when Jesus was teaching His disciples about faith and extending forgiveness, they asked

Jesus for an increase of faith. Jesus responded by comparing faith to a mustard seed (Luke 17:5). It is not so much about the size of the mustard seed, but its character. A mustard seed, though tiny, grows tremendously over time and with care. Your faith is the same. Your faith grows as you guard it and exercise it. Jesus says your faith will increase if it is like the mustard seed. Though small in the beginning, the mustard seed becomes strong and it responds to care. The stronger your confidence in the character of God, the more your faith will grow.

Consider the exchange Jesus had with His disciples about faith and the mustard seed.

If your brother sins and disregards God's precepts, solemnly warn him; and if he repents and changes, forgive him. Even if he sins against you seven times a day, and returns to you seven times and says, 'I repent,' you must forgive him [that is, give up resentment and consider the offense recalled and annulled]." The apostles said to the Lord, "Increase our faith [our ability to confidently trust in God and in His power]." And the Lord said, "If you have [confident, abiding] faith in God [even as small] as a mustard seed, you could say to this mulberry tree [which has very strong roots], 'Be pulled up by the roots and be planted in the sea'; and [if the request was

*in agreement with the will of God] it would
have obeyed you.* (Luke 17:4-6, AMP).

What is faith? Faith is belief. To have faith is to
have confidence in the appearance of something you
do not yet see. We cannot see God with our natural
eyes, yet we believe He exists. We have faith that He
hears and answers prayer. When you sit to read and
study your Bible, for example, you may pray first
and ask God to speak to your heart through His word
and give you the ability to understand what you are
reading. By faith you then pick up your Bible and
begin to read. You believe in your heart that God has
heard your prayer and you listen with your heart for
a word from Him as you read.

Faith is more a conviction than an emotion. We
may not always feel like forgiving, but once we
decide in our hearts to forgive, we believe God for
the grace to do so.

Grace empowers you to do what you could not
do on your own. Some of life's experiences have
hurt so deeply perhaps that only the Holy Spirit can
give you the grace to forgive. Ask the Holy Spirit to
help you to forgive. Cry to Him about your hurt and
let the Holy Spirit comfort you. As you look to the
Holy Spirit for comfort and peace, He will help you
to let go of the hatred and bitterness and resentment
and anger toward those who hurt you. He does this
by loving you out of brokenness into wholeness.
God wants us to forgive others just as He has

forgiven us through the Blood of Jesus Christ. You and I did not deserve to be forgiven, but God chose to forgive us our sins. People who have hurt you may not deserve to be forgiven, but God asks you to choose to forgive them.

Many times, we equate forgiveness with restoration. To forgive someone does not mean restoration, necessarily. Forgiveness means simply that you release the person in your heart from the emotional debt they owe you. When you forgive someone, it is you who are freed. Trust God to make up to you what you lost or what was taken from you. Roman 12:19 tells us. *"Dearly beloved, avenge not yourselves, but rather give place unto wrath: for it is written, Vengeance is mine; I will repay, saith the Lord"* (KJV).

Many concentrate on this scripture with hope that God will repay one's enemies with some misfortune attuned to the pain they caused, but I believe God will repay *you* - that is - give *you* justice for what you have suffered. Many times, our hesitation with forgiveness is the belief that someone is getting away or that we are losing without remedy, but not so with God. God will repay *you*. He will make up to you all the pain and injustice you have suffered in your life. You can let go of the anger and let the Holy Spirit comfort and heal you. Forgiveness is not always a feeling. Forgiveness, like love, is a decision. Decide to trust the Holy Spirit to make up to you for all you have lost.

A major temptation you will find relief in overcoming is the inclination toward self-condemnation, the shame and guilt arising from past or present sin. Condemnation is akin to judgment and the pronouncement of death. But, the law of the spirit of life in Christ Jesus has made us free from the law of sin and death. *"So now there is no condemnation for those who belong to Christ Jesus. And because you belong to him, the power of the life-giving Spirit has freed you from the power of sin that leads to death"*(Romans 8:1). Remember, the scriptures reveal that anyone who is in Christ Jesus is a new creature. Old things are passed away and all things are become new. We refrain from judging others and we do not condemn - that is pass the judgment of death upon ourselves.

> *Either way, Christ's love controls us. Since we believe that Christ died for all, we also believe that we have all died to our old life. He died for everyone so that those who receive his new life will no longer live for themselves. Instead, they will live for Christ, who died and was raised for them. So we have stopped evaluating others from a human point of view. At one time we thought of Christ merely from a human point of view. How differently we know him now! This means that anyone who belongs to Christ has become a new person. The old life is gone; a new life has begun!*
> (II Corinthians 5:17).

We endeavor, by God's grace, to live without sinning. However, because we are human, we fall short. The Holy Spirit convicts us of sin. He speaks to our hearts to let us know that we have sinned. We may have to ask someone's forgiveness for something we have said or done. We may need to change some behavior that is displeasing to God or hindering to our growth as Christians. In any case, we heed the instruction of the Holy Spirit without sinking into shame. Commit this scripture to memory.

> *But if we are living in the light, as God is in the light, then we have fellowship with each other, and the blood of Jesus, his Son, cleanses us from all sin. If we claim we have no sin, we are only fooling ourselves and not living in the truth. But if we confess our sins to him, he is faithful and just to forgive us our sins and to cleanse us from all wickedness* (I John 1:7-9).

Guard Your Gates

"For we are not fighting against flesh-and-blood enemies, but against evil rulers and authorities of the unseen world, against mighty powers in this dark world, and against evil spirits in the heavenly places."

"Therefore, put on every piece of God's armor so you will be able to resist the enemy in the time of evil. Then after the battle you will still be standing firm."

- Ephesians 6:12-13

Gates are entryways. Gates may designed for protection. Gates may also be designed to prevent freedom. You are a spiritual being living in a body made of flesh. The sin nature within us attempts to rule through the flesh. Have you ever heard the expression, the spirit is willing but the flesh is weak? The Bible lets us know about the ways the flesh desires to act in ways that are contrary to the spirt.

The sinful nature wants to do evil, which is just the opposite of what the Spirit wants. And the Spirit gives us desires that are the opposite of what the sinful nature desires. These two forces are constantly fighting each other, so you are not free to carry out your good intentions. (Galatians 5:17).

There are times, for example, when you will sense a leading to pray or study your Bible, and just when you are thinking about getting started, your body will send you a thought like, *"I'm tired, maybe tomorrow."* You may wake up ready to attend worship services and your body will send you a thought like, *"I can watch worship online or on television. I'm tired. I don't need to go out."*

You may be attending worship services regularly, when one day you are offered overtime or someone requests you to work at the time you would normally attend worship. A thought may enter your mind like, *"God knows I love Him. He knows my heart. God is giving me this opportunity to make the money I need to further my career."* All kinds of excuses may come to your mind to lure you away from worship services or the closeness of your relationship with your Heavenly Father. Let no thing and no one keep you away from worship services. Hebrews 10:25 reminds us of the importance of worshipping together. *"And let us not neglect our meeting together, as some people do, but encourage one another, especially now that the day of his return is drawing near."*

Carnality is the state of being ruled by the flesh. You may have heard the term carnal Christians. You do not want to be a carnal Christian. Carnal

Christians are people who profess to know Christ but their lifestyles are just like those of the world. A carnal Christian is someone you would not recognize immediately as a Christian by their behaviors, choices, lifestyles or conversations. Carnal Christians are in love with the world and everything the world has to offer. Carnal Christians share the world's value system and value the things of the world. Consider I John 2:16. *"For the world offers only a craving for physical pleasure, a craving for everything we see, and pride in our achievements and possessions. These are not from the Father, but are from this world."*

Carnal Christians are people who profess to accept Jesus Christ as their Savior but who do not allow Jesus to be Lord in their lives. Carnal Christians retain the position of lord for themselves to live and do what they want, how they want, when they want and why they want. When faced with the challenge of choice, the carnal Christian chooses her will and desires over that which is pleasing to Christ. The carnal Christian, not Jesus, is seated on the throne of the carnal Christian's heart.

You may have heard of Jesus fasting for 40 days and being tempted by the devil as Luke describes in Luke 4:1-13.

Then Jesus, full of the Holy Spirit, returned from the Jordan River. He was led by the Spirit in the wilderness, where he was tempted by the devil for forty days. Jesus ate nothing all that time and became very hungry. Then the devil said to him, "If you are the Son of God, tell this stone to become a loaf of bread." But Jesus told him, "No! The Scriptures say, 'People do not live by bread alone.'" Then the devil took him up and revealed to him all the kingdoms of the world in a moment of time. "I will give you the glory of these kingdoms and authority over them," the devil said, "because they are mine to give to anyone I please. I will give it all to you if you will worship me."

Jesus replied, "The Scriptures say, 'You must worship the your God and serve only him.'" Then the devil took him to Jerusalem, to the highest point of the Temple, and said, "If you are the Son of God, jump off! For the Scriptures say, 'He will order his angels to protect and guard you. And they will hold you up with their hands so you won't even hurt your foot on a stone.'" Jesus responded, "The Scriptures also say, 'You must not test the Lord your God.'" When the devil had finished tempting Jesus, he left him until the next opportunity came.

During that period of temptation by the devil, Jesus demonstrated what it is like to be faced with choices and reasonings that attempt to take

Christians off the path of righteousness. The devil tried to convince Jesus, who was hungry indeed, to take matters into His own hands by turning stones into bread.

Be cautioned that the devil will try to send thoughts to you directly or suggestions through others to take matters into your own hands when you know your Heavenly Father has a purpose for where you are as well as a set time for your change to come.

Jesus told the devil and His message is for us today. It is never about exerting power because we have it or looking constantly for ways to satisfy the lusts of the flesh. It is about seeking God and His will for our lives, whether in the simplest or most dire of circumstances.

The devil tried to tempt Jesus with riches and the power that goes along with them. The devil's only requirement was that Jesus bow down and worship him. Be cautioned that many today are worshipping money, fame and power. Whatever a person is pursuing with all their might indicates where the person's heart is. The whole earth belongs to the Lord and all that is in it. *"The earth is the LORD 's, and everything in it. The world and all its people belong to him. For he laid the earth's foundation on the seas and built it on the ocean depths"* (Psalm 24:1-2). The devil tried to sell Jesus something that Jesus already owns!

Be cautioned, Beloved, that the devil will try to get you to give up your faith to go after things that already belong to you. Your Heavenly Father is your provider and has already promised to take care of all things that concern you. You do not have to lose your health or family or peace trying to pursue that which already belongs to you. Not only that, it is not God's will for us to seek riches for prideful display. If pride is the motive, the price one pays will be far too dear. The flesh, through its eyes, will lust after anything that makes it feel powerful, superior and in charge.

Your Heavenly Father wants you to be blessed, undoubtedly. However, He does not want you to worship money or compromise your convictions by chasing after it at any cost. Do not allow the devil to make you chase and bow to him for what already belongs to you. *"Once I was young, and now I am old. Yet I have never seen the godly abandoned or their children begging for bread. For the LORD loves justice, and he will never abandon the godly[...]"* (Psalm 37:25, 28a).

Bow down to no person and no thing to get want you want. Bow only to your Heavenly Father, who alone is worthy of worship and praise. Remember always that your Heavenly Father, who spared not His own Son, but gave Him up for us all, will also with Him freely give us all things. *"Since he did not spare even his own Son but gave him up for us all, won't he also give us everything else?"* (Romans 8:32).

When the devil could not succeed in tempting Jesus in other ways, the devil tried to convince Jesus to jump off a high point of the temple. Jesus could see right through the devil who tried to make Jesus operate in pride. Pride may try to get you to assert yourself when you do not have to in order to prove something to someone. The devil attempted to convince Jesus to venture outside of His divine purpose for being where He was. The devil tried to convince Jesus to venture out of His station with God. *"Don't make rash promises, and don't be hasty in bringing matters before God. After all, God is in heaven, and you are here on earth. So let your words be few"* (Ecclesiastes 5:2). *"The fear of the LORD is the beginning of wisdom: a good understanding have all they that do his commandments..."* (Psalm 111:10a).

These three temptations will arise throughout your life:

✝ the temptation to take matters into your own hands - to make something happen on your own when you have a legitimate need that is going unfulfilled

There is nothing wrong with being proactive or actively pursuing one's dreams or desires, however, the Bible cautions Christians to discern the difference between working hard to bring dreams to reality and manipulating circumstances and /or people to get in the present what God has planned for the future.

✝ the temptation to pursue riches or fame or anything that promises fulfillment or the superficial appearance of it in place of a genuine relationship with God – to follow the world's lead in gaining all the latest material things

God wants you to prosper and be in health *even as your soul prospers. "Beloved, I pray that in every way you may succeed and prosper and be in good health [physically], just as [I know] your soul prospers [spiritually]* (III John 1, AMP). The key, beloved, is that prosperity of soul, which is strength of character developed by spiritual maturity, empowers you to keep first things first – that is the pursuit of Christ and fellowship with Him. Relationship with Christ should be foremost pursuit in the life of a Christian. Did you know that worldly treasures and wealth do not count in heaven's value system? Consider the words of Jesus. "And if you are untrustworthy about worldly wealth, who will trust you with the true riches of heaven?

✝ the temptation to prove yourself by exuding undo confidence in your own abilities in your own time and at your own whim – the temptation to acquire material things or flaunt accomplishments to look good in front of other people

These are a few of the experiences that are common to Christians. The Bible cautions us to heed the leading of the Spirit and not give in to the flesh because the one to whom we attach the greatest priority will have rule and dominion in our lives. It is impossible to mature in Christ if we are indulging the flesh at every turn.

As Christians, we have to pay close attention to what and to whom we allow to have influence in our lives. Every choice we make impacts us spiritually. Something as simple as what we chose to watch online or on television affects us spiritually. Our eyes are a kind of gate through which influence flows. What we allow our eyes to behold or take in can cause us to win or lose a battle in our flesh – which begins in the mind. Whatever enters through the gates heads toward the mind to get the mind to cause the body to act.

Our gates can be akin to our senses. We are flesh and blood and, as such, sensual in nature. We perceive through our senses. We experience most of the pleasures we derive through our senses. Our bodies react to what the senses experience. How often have you felt hungry immediately upon sensing the fragrance of cookies freshly baked? God gave us our senses to assist us in avoiding danger, but also for our enjoyment. How beautiful is it to behold a natural wonder like a mountain range or a family of deer or a pelican? Have you ever been awakened by the melodious sounds of birds singing?

Just as there beautiful feelings we experience through our senses, there are also negative influences that attempt to enter our hearts and minds through our senses. I heard someone say once that listening to a certain type of music made him angry. Music is known to affect the state of mind and influence the mood. It has been said that listening to certain music influenced individuals to take actions they later regretted. When we allow, not just negative music, but negative language to enter in, it affects us spiritually. We become less attuned to the Spirit of God when are ears are filled with profanity and worldliness, including gossip.

Our eyes and ears are only two of the ports of entry where negativity and deception attempt to influence our minds. We have to be careful what we touch and what or whom we allow to touch us. Touching illegal or other harmful drugs, for example, may not keep you from heaven, but they may get you there a lot sooner than God intends for you to arrive.

Certain relationships that do not honor your Heavenly Father do not honor who you are in Christ. While the relationship, itself, may not be bad, certain aspects of the relationship may be unhealthy or out of order. Let no one convince you that God's way, as outlined in the Bible, is old fashioned and not for today. That is a lie from the devil. When God outlines standards and order for relationships, He does so to protect you, not to keep anything good away from you. When we are joined with another person, we become one spiritually. If that relationship is not sanctioned by God, its influence impedes our spiritual growth and maturity in Christ.

Remember, just as the devil tried to tempt Jesus to focus on His flesh at the expense of His divine calling and purpose, the devil will try to tempt you. God will never tempt you. God may test you, but temptation will never come from God. James 1:12-17 explains.

> *God blesses those who patiently endure testing and temptation. Afterward they will receive the crown of life that God has promised to those who love him. And remember, when you are being tempted, do not say, "God is tempting me." God is never tempted to do wrong, and he never tempts anyone else. Temptation comes from our own desires, which entice us and drag us away. These desires give birth to sinful actions. And when sin is allowed to grow, it gives birth to death. So don't be misled, my dear brothers and sisters. Whatever is good and perfect is a gift coming down to us from God our Father, who created all the lights*

*in the heavens. He never changes or casts a
shifting shadow.*

Focus On God's Approval

"Make it your goal to live a quiet life, minding your own business..."

- 1 Thessalonians 4:11

"Do your best to present yourself to God as one approved, a worker who does not need to be ashamed and who correctly handles the word of truth"

- II Timothy 2:15
New International Version (NIV)

Most of the scripture references in this book are from the New Living Translation of the Bible. There are many translations of the Bible. Translations I have in my library include the King James Version of the Bible, the New Living Translation, the Amplified Bible and the New International Version of the Bible. You may choose to obtain a study Bible at some point. I have found that a good study Bible will offer cross referencing of verses as well as topic categories for study throughout the scriptures. The reason a good study Bible offers cross referencing of scriptures is because the Bible interprets itself. Always remember that. A good study Bible will show you a cross sampling of scriptures containing particular subjects, lessons or words. If you want to study the life of Jesus, for example, a good study

Bible will list several scriptures outlining the genealogy, chronology, ministry, miracles, life, death, and resurrection of Jesus. A study Bible will also show you many scriptures about Jesus and God's plan for humankind's salvation beginning in the Old Testament with Genesis, A good study Bible will help you to see how the whole Bible is about Jesus and God's love for people. There are many good study Bibles. My first and favorite study Bible still is the Thompson Chain Reference Bible.

There are a few books you should make a part of your library as a Christian. *Scripture Keys for Kingdom Living*, compiled by June Newman Davis, is a thorough book of scriptures categorized for prayer and study on various subjects.[1] You can reference this booklet to familiarize yourself with God's word as it pertains to specific topics from faith to healing and more. *Scripture Keys for Kingdom Living,* is a great resource for prayer as well. You may feel apprehensive about praying, especially in the beginning. But be assured that while people make judgments based on one's outward appearance or performance, God judges the heart. Utilize the Scriptures to pray God's word back to Him.

As you begin a deeper study of God's word, consider adding a Bible concordance and Bible dictionary to your library. Because the Bible was

---

[1] Scripture Keys Ministries, PO Box 6559, Denver, Colorado 80206-0559. 1-303-333-1034. ScriptureKeys.com

originally written in ancient Hebrew, Aramaic and Greek, a good concordance can enhance your understanding of certain words and phrases as originally written. I like to refer to the *Strong's Exhaustive Concordance of the Bible* by James Strong (available in hard copy and online). There are many Bible dictionaries from which to choose. I recommend taking the time to browse through a good portion until you find one you like best. There are many Bible commentaries available as well. Be cautioned that while Bible commentaries are plentiful, they are varied and few may be really Holy Spirit inspired and trustworthy. I have the Matthew Henry Bible Commentary as a part of my library. Many Bible resources are available at your local Christian bookstore and online for your convenience.

It is a good idea to limit your inquiry and study to the Bible and other Bible based materials at this time. While other religious materials may seem interesting and intriguing, especially those offering insight into books or topics described as left out of the Bible, confusion can easily set in when attempting to reconcile philosophical viewpoints on spirituality, God and the life and significance of Jesus Christ. There are many religions that acknowledge Jesus as significant or as a prophet, however, not as the one and only Son of God as the Bible clearly states Jesus is. John 3:16 is the foundation upon which our faith is built. *"For God so loved the world that he gave his one and only Son, that whoever believes in him shall not perish but have eternal life."*

As a new Christian, it is important that you get to know your Bible and make the truth of God's word as written in your Bible the standard by which you measure the validity of all other books or beliefs. Despite New Age and other contemporary teachings, all roads **do not** lead to the same god Neither do Christians and believers in other religions worship the same god.

Always remember John14:6, *"Jesus told him, 'I am the way, the truth, and the life. No one can come to the Father except through me.'"* Commit this to your heart and memory and let nothing and no one move you away from the Truth, who is Jesus Christ, the only begotten Son of God, the Father. When tempted to doubt, repeat this in your heart and say aloud, *Jesus is Lord. The Lord He is God and God is my Father.*

This is my prayer to the Father for you.

Dear Father in Heaven, I thank You for Your beloved one who has come to accept Your grace today. I thank You that You have delivered Your child out of darkness and translated Your child into the kingdom of Your dear Son. I pray, Father, that You lead and guide Your child by the love and grace of Your Holy Spirit. Baptize and fill Your child to the utmost with the Holy Spirit and let no enemy in flesh or spirit interfere with the plan, purpose and destiny You have for Your child. May the Holy Spirit be Your child's constant companion, protector, provider, healer, comforter and friend. Cause the peace of God, which passes all understanding to keep Your child's heart and mind through Christ Jesus. Father, in the name of Your Son and our Savior, the Lord Jesus Christ, I pray that You give Your child complete knowledge of Your will along with all spiritual wisdom and understanding. I pray for the Holy Spirit to empower Your child to live in a way that will always honor and please You, Lord, and Your child's life will produce every kind of good fruit, all the while your child is growing and learning to know You, Father, better and better. I pray that You strengthen Your child with all Your glorious power so Your child will have all the endurance and patience Your child needs. May Your child be filled with joy, always thanking You, Father, who has enabled Your child to share in the inheritance that belongs to Your people, who live in the light. Cause Your child to never doubt but always remain confident that, no matter what, Your thoughts and plans for Your child are always good and not of evil to give Your child a future and a hope. Bless You, Father. I pray this prayer and ask these blessings upon Your child this day in the name above all names, Jesus Christ, Your only begotten Son and our Savior because of Your grace. Amen.

Thank you, Beloved, for taking the time to read this book and open your heart to Jesus Christ. Today, you have made the best decision of your life by accepting Jesus Christ as your Lord and Savior. Begin reading your Bible and attending church right away. Good places to begin reading your Bible are with Genesis, the first book of the Bible, and the Gospel of John in the New Testament. I recommend beginning with the New International Version (NIV), the New Living Translation (NLT) or the Amplified version of the Bible (AMP) as each utilizes modern language to help you understand Bible principles without deciphering ancient use of text. I grew up with the King James Version and it remains my favorite although I read and study with the above mentioned texts for clarity and understanding. If you are new to reading and studying the Bible, the modern texts mentioned are great to begin your journey. The Bible is God's love letter to you. Reading and studying your Bible will help you to get to know your Savior and apply Biblical principles to your life and choices.

Always remember that God's love for you is unconditional and there are no qualifiers nor conditions for His love. God loves you because He created you in His image and likeness for His glory. Commit Ephesians 2:8-10 to your heart.

God saved you by his grace when you believed. And you can't take credit for this; it is a gift from God. Salvation is not a

*reward for the good things we have done,
so none of us can boast about it. For we
are God's masterpiece. He has created us
anew in Christ Jesus, so we can do the good
things he planned for us long ago.*

There is no sin you have committed in your past
or will commit now or in the future that can diminish
God's love for you. We are human and prone to sin,
but we do not have to live in sin. When we sin, we
can repent- that is to turn away from the sin – and
ask for forgiveness. *"If we claim we have no sin, we
are only fooling ourselves and not living in the truth.
But if we confess our sins to him, he is faithful and
just to forgive us our sins and to cleanse us from all
wickedness"* (I John 1:9-10).

Keep in mind, Beloved, that the forgiveness of
God is a manifestation of His divine grace toward us.
Although we appreciate God's grace, we cannot, in
good conscience, make a practice or lifestyle of
sinning just because we know God will forgive us, or
extend His grace toward us. The devil will try to
deceive you into willful sin as a practice with the
assurance of God's grace.

*Well then, should we keep on sinning so
that God can show us more and more of his
wonderful grace? Of course not! Since we
have died to sin, how can we continue to*

*live in it? [...] We know that our old sinful
selves were crucified with Christ so that sin
might lose its power in our lives. We are no
longer slaves to sin. For when we died with
Christ we were set free from the power of
sin.* (Romans 6:1-2, 6-7).

Remember, Beloved, that you have been set free
not from the penalty of sin only, but from the power
of sin. Sin can no longer rule over you or dictate
your life, thoughts or actions at will. This is not to
say that you will not make mistakes. This *is* to say,
however, that you are no longer bound to a lifestyle
of sin.

*Those who have been born into God's
family do not make a practice of sinning,
because God's life is in them. So they can't
keep on sinning, because they are children
of God. So now we can tell who are
children of God and who are children of the
devil. Anyone who does not live righteously
and does not love other believers does not
belong to God* (I John 3:9-10).

Let us practice thankfulness for the grace of God.
*"...Rejoice because your names are registered in
heaven"* (Luke 10:20b).

*God saved you by his grace when you
believed. And you can't take credit for this;
it is a gift from God. Salvation is not a*

*reward for the good things we have done,
so none of us can boast about it. For we are
God's masterpiece. He has created us anew
in Christ Jesus, so we can do the good
things he planned for us long ago.*

Nothing can separate you from God's love for you.

*And I am convinced that nothing can ever
separate us from God's love. Neither death
nor life, neither angels nor demons, neither
our fears for today nor our worries about
tomorrow - not even the powers of hell can
separate us from God's love. No power in
the sky above or in the earth below -
indeed, nothing in all creation will ever be
able to separate us from the love of God
that is revealed in Christ Jesus our Lord*
(Romans 8:38-39).

The reality of the Cross and the redemptive
Blood Jesus Christ shed for us are true forever.

*The message of the cross is foolish to those
who are headed for destruction! But we
who are being saved know it is the very
power of God* (I Corinthians 1:18).

*Without question, this is the great mystery
of our faith: Christ was revealed in a
human body and vindicated by the Spirit.
He was seen by angels and announced to*

the nations. He was believed in throughout the world and taken to heaven in glory (I Timothy 3:16).

Today, I gave my heart to Jesus.

Date of my Salvation:

_____ _____ _____

Today is the first day of the best of your life!

God's blessings rest upon you as you walk with Christ. Stay encouraged and know that I am praying for you always.

Love in Christ,
Bonny

Notes

Notes

More books by Bonny V. Banks

Hospital Visitation Handbook for Ministers

Hospital Visitation Guide for Ministers

Manual del ministro para visitor hospitales

*Leader Reach: Essays on the Dynamics of
Communication, Values, Spirituality and
Power in Leadership*

He Would Rather Die Than Live Without You

www.ingramcontent.com/pod-product-compliance
Lightning Source LLC
Chambersburg PA
CBHW061753020426
42331CB00006B/1466